GOING THROUGH

Lillyan Jiles

GOING THROUGH
Copyright © 2020 by Lillyan Jiles

DEDICATION

I dedicate this book to my daughters
Ajahanà and Lexes.
It is a testament to the giants that were slayed for you and
a reminder that you hold within you that same power.
Remember to slay in Jesus' name!

~

I would also like to dedicate this book to the women now, girls then,
who held me down.
We endured a lot and I know I would not have made it without you,
my sisters.
I pray you will release your own stories so your hearts will be healed.
I love you always.

TABLE OF CONTENTS

INTRODUCTION

First, I want to thank you for joining me on this journey through my life. It is my prayer that my journey will inspire you to go on your own journey. A journey into the mindsets that make you who you are. I hope you discover, as I did, your own falsehoods or wrong thought patterns. It has been my experience that these wrong mindsets can result from traumatic experiences from the past or could have been passed down to you from previous generations. The key to identifying these false mindsets can be found after you have analyzed your life, particularly the areas not bearing good fruit. When I say, "bearing good fruit," I mean the areas in your life where you have strived, but could not achieve your planned or desired level of accomplishment. Those areas that, no matter how hard you tried, never seemed to come out the way you envisioned.

I know the frustration and lack of motivation wrong thought patterns can cause. The results of the trauma I experienced in my childhood continued to show up and affected my future until I made a conscious decision not to hide them anymore. I didn't want to hide all the things that were done to me or continue to make excuses for the things I did to others. Those things were the results of fear and shame. I had to face it. I once heard a pastor use the acronym H.O.T. during his sermon, which he said stood for humble, open, and transparent. Coincidently that was precisely what I had to become. I was so angry that I had let my past rob me of the future I knew I deserved. I learned that what we keep in the dark or sweep under the rug can never be resolved so we can heal. I could not see the damage for what it really was because I was making excuses to continue to cover it up. It should make you so angry you are not living the life you deserve that

9

you become H.O.T. (humble, open, transparent) as well.

Once these traumas were uncovered, it was my responsibility to take ownership of them. My trauma and all that came after was a part of me. Whether I liked it or not, it contributed to my life and had as much influence as the things that were good and intentional. Taking ownership makes it my problem and my responsibility to handle. I discovered that *I* was the change that had to be made.

I couldn't change others or even force them to see things my way. I had to change myself and the wrong thought processes that had come together and somehow made sense in my mind. To do that, I had to get to the bottom, or should I say, "the beginning." I had to find the answers to some critical questions to see things clearly. Where did that thought begin? What did it stem from? How has it hindered my progress? What can I learn from it moving forward? These and a few other hard questions had to be answered.

When we are young, we plan how we want our lives to be. We think about the kind of job we will have and the type of house we plan to live in. We think about the spouse we want and how many children we want to have. We all have areas of our lives that have not reached the potential we once thought they could have. Finding out *why* became my mission and fueled my motivation to seek and find the root cause of my lack of achievement in those areas. I was tired of fruitless efforts. Once the root is uncovered, we can then change the wrong mindset. Some wrong mindsets have roots too deep to uncover. This is the case when they are generational. In these cases, we must be willing to disconnect ourselves from that vein by rejecting the lie and then establishing new truths for ourselves.

Finally, I had to deal with the consequences of my decisions. Some decisions are made for us, and we don't get a say, especially as a child. I went through things and was put in situations that were beyond my control. I didn't pick my mother or father and didn't choose the circumstances I was raised in. In my mind, that gave me every right to blame everyone else for how my life had turned out. The choices *I* made for myself became their fault as well. I had to learn where to draw the line. How long was I going to *decide* to let my past predict my future? Unfortunately, I cannot control the things that other people did to me in the past. I had to open my eyes to see that I do have control over how I respond to them. There are some things I have done in response to what was done to me. Some decisions and choices I made seemed like the best options in my broken state. Facing those things was not easy, but admitting my wrongs somehow made everything right.

The process was more complicated than it sounds in theory because I often got in my own way. We tend to look at the fruitless areas of our lives and become depressed, discouraged, and some of us decide not to deal with them at all. The problem with that approach is things we don't confront will never change and will continue to confront us. I kept doing the same things, hoping for different results. Worst of all, I became complacent with those areas and accepted the level where I had plateaued, instead of striving for what I needed, wanted, and felt like I deserved. I had learned to settle. I settled for where I was and simply lived day to day. I was content with just being able to make it through the day. I wasn't planning for a future that looked better. I was just getting by.

I had planned a life with a husband, a couple of kids and a dog in a beautiful home. An experience like the ones I saw portrayed on TV in *The Cosby Show*, *Full House*, and *Family Matters*. Those shows were centered around families that honored, respected, protected and loved each other. My vision was a life that was the opposite of the one I grew up in. I clung to a relationship with a man six years my senior, even after it became abusive. I didn't know any better, and I was holding on to an unrealistic idea of a family. We had children together, and I wanted my children to have the two-parent home I didn't. That was one of the reasons I kept going back, the other was the fear of actually being a single parent. I wanted my family together and even begged him to marry me.

By the time he decided to do me that favor, I was fed up with all the fighting and having to defend myself constantly. That whole relationship is a book by itself that I may just write one day. It was a storm full of blessings and lessons. If you ever get through a difficult season in your life without any lessons, you are liable to have to repeat it. The blessing is not always found in the exhale of making it through. Most of the time, it's in the lessons you were supposed to collect along the way.

Those of us who have become accustomed to our wrong mindsets have made room for them, and at some point decided they weren't that much of an issue, so we adjusted to them. This is a wrong mindset in itself. The "no big deal" things do affect you. It's like having a hangnail. It's something small and may seem insignificant in the grand scheme of things. I mean, many of us wouldn't see a doctor for it. Yet it can cause a considerable amount of pain and become such an annoyance that we are willing to, without thinking, rip the hangnail off using our teeth. We are not thinking about the pain that will follow when that thing has annoyed and frustrated us all day. We become more determined to get rid of it by any means necessary rather than take care of it properly. We can't afford to take that approach with our wrong thought processes. No matter how insignificant they may seem, they affect us daily.

"Write a book? For what? Who's going to read it?" Those were my questions when my therapist sat back in her chair, removed her glasses, looked me straight in the eye and said, "You need to write a book." I was almost halfway through telling her my life story, which by then I had condensed into a 45-minute summary due to the one-hour session time. I prided myself on being able to leave 15 minutes for questions or just a moment for the therapist to catch her breath.

I have never had a problem talking about the things that have happened in my life. I felt it was the only way someone could really get to know me. I'd seen so many therapists, it was getting easier to tell the story over and over. Although sometimes accompanied by tears, the story made me who I was and could help them understand me better. Never considered it could help me understand myself better. So I would breeze through it as if I were talking about someone else's life. I always knew my past held keys to understanding some things better; I just felt like it was too overwhelming to dig up.

The therapist's statement caught me by surprise and puzzled me at first. She explained that the book wouldn't be for others to read. I was to use it to help me confront feelings I had been suppressing. She was after the pain, anger, and fear that was connected to the past I was avoiding. She explained that writing things down would change my perspective. If I could look at my life from an analytical viewpoint, I could recognize and change behaviors that resulted from the traumas.

During the next several years, I began to write all the horrible experiences that had happened to me with all the details I could remember. I wouldn't suggest anyone with a past like mine should do this without adequate support. When you begin to deal with traumatic incidents in your life, you need another perspective; yours will be clouded by your feelings and judgment. The takeaway is that you must deal with the trauma in your life, or it will continue to hinder you. You never totally suppress traumatic childhood memories. Even if you can't recall the event, the effects will show up in your behavior. Those writings became this book's first draft. Over the years, I have used that first draft to answer that *why* question. I really wanted to change and have the life I felt I deserved, but even with all my best efforts, it continued to elude me.

When we can learn to view our lives with an analytical eye, we can detach ourselves from the feelings and emotions connected to it and make choices based on logic. This process is the answer to the question of why you can give such good advice to others but cannot apply it to yourself. This is because of your viewpoint. You are so close you can't see where or how to apply the solution. Think of a picture. When you are in the picture, you have a different viewpoint than the person taking the picture. If you step outside the image, you can then see the changes that need to be made to improve the picture. I had to step out of the image of my life. By disconnecting myself from the pain and trauma that paralyzed me, I could see how I developed some toxic mindsets and also discovered some ways to change them.

It is my disclaimer that although I have a degree in psychology, this knowledge I share is based on personal experience. I may use some psychological terms and rationales. Still, my goal is to allow you to find your own revelations within my personal story and journey. Although I experienced a multitude of traumatic events in my life, I am not naive enough to think one person's life experiences could hold answers for everyone. I hope you find strength from my story to apply the process to your own areas of struggle. While I am not a theologian, pastor, or spiritual leader, I am someone who has been in a relationship with Jesus Christ for over 30 years, speaking about what I know has worked for me and countless others. It is because of Him that I am sharing my life with you so transparently, with the hope that someone will find help and healing for their own.

CHAPTER 1:
WRITING THE WRONGS

Writing this book first afforded me the ability to detach myself from the pain of my past and see the wrong mindsets. Second, the ability to know how those mindsets have affected me and others helped me to shed the victim mentality and see how I had victimized others. This also helped me to forgive the people who hurt me because I recognized all the people *I* had hurt. Third, opening myself up in such a vulnerable way is stripping away insecurities, shame, and pride. No one but Jesus knows this person I'm about to reveal.

Anyone who knows me won't recognize this version of me because I've protected her. By shielding her from the world, I also shielded her from the light of truth. Unconditional love is found there. I have learned that it's not my job to coddle and protect her. It never was. I needed to let go of her and let God do His job. I needed to release her to Him. He has the power to take all that was bad and use it for good. Now I have released it all to Him with the expectation that He will use all the bad to continue to grow me and save another. I pray healing, deliverance, and freedom will erupt from this testimony and bless somebody in more ways than it continues to bless me.

This book has uprooted some pain from deep within me and will surface some pain in others. It is never my goal to inflict pain, but it is often necessary for real healing to begin. The pain we suppress festers, and it eats at us from the inside out. There are some people tied to my past who have not dealt with their skeletons. Because of this I have chosen not to use names. But it's only when we confront the deep-seated issues of our past instead of ignoring them, that we can begin to heal ourselves and help others to do the same.

Let me be clear, my reason for sharing *my* traumatic incidents is to expose the root or birthplace of my mindsets, not the people connected to them. I'm sorry if my truths make anyone feel uneasy or shine a light on a version of yourself you are not yet acquainted with. If my story affects you in this manner, it is a clear indication that you may need to take your own journey. It is my prayer that through my transparency, others will gain the strength to see their own stories from a different viewpoint and seek the truth that leads to victory in their lives.

When my therapist told me to write a book, I understood the emotional toll of this undertaking. I specifically remember her telling me to use as much detail as I could remember about the incidents. I was reluctant to dig up all the trauma I had buried so many years ago, in an attempt to live what she called, "a better life." But I realized I was not living the life I had planned for myself. I was experiencing the anger, fear, and anxiety I tried to escape by burying my past. I know now I was only hurting myself as contentment and joy escaped me daily. I know that God has promised life abundantly. I wasn't living that promise. Do you live that promised life? Do you want to?

At that point in my life, I was diagnosed with agoraphobia, which is an anxiety disorder characterized by an irrational fear of open places. It started with panic attacks. The attacks occurred when I was out in public places and would come on without a trigger. I limited the amount of time I spent outside of the house trying to avoid having panic attacks in public. I felt embarrassed by the attention I received whenever I had an attack. The stares, the pointing, and many times people crowded around trying to help. If you have ever had a panic attack, you know the feeling of not being able to breathe.

The attention only raised the level of my anxiety and prolonged the attack. It became more comfortable to just stay in. If I absolutely had to leave the house, like for a doctor's appointment, I would wear a robe. This particular robe was big, fluffy, and cranberry-colored. No matter the temperature, I wore that robe every time I had to go outside. I'm sure I brought more attention to myself in that robe than the panic attacks did. I must have looked ridiculous now that I think about it. It had become my security blanket, and it made me feel safe from the outside world like I was being held. I needed it at that time because the life I planned and tried to build had fallen apart around me.

I had been a single parent for almost 10 years and hadn't even taken a moment to figure out my life. I had tunnel vision and was just doing whatever I needed to do to feed, clothe, and provide shelter for my kids. I never even looked up to notice I was doing the very thing I was so afraid I couldn't do. I was working and providing for my family on my own. When I finally got the strength to leave that relationship and was fed up enough not to go back, I went to school, got my CNA certification, and got a job. I worked in a nursing home for 5 years before I got my first private duty client. I was killing myself working 80 hours a week, trying to keep both jobs. The nursing home provided benefits and job security, but private duty paid more. I ended up choosing private duty and letting God secure me. I developed three rules that led to job security.

Never call off. Be there when you are scheduled and work everything else in your life around that schedule.

Show up on time. Arriving when your shift starts is not on time, that's late.

Most important, work harder than your replacement. Everyone is expendable.

Because of these three rules and the grace of God, I have never been without a job opportunity.

I was working as a private duty caregiver, just making ends meet but still providing for my family, and then my client of five years passed away. When you work in private care, you get to know your clients personally; they become like family. I was so close to this family they offered to let us rent one of their houses and I accepted. I knew it was so I could be closer in proximity to them, with the house located behind theirs, but I was grateful. It was a beautiful house in one of the friendliest neighborhoods I had ever lived in. I was so proud to be able to provide such a nice place for my girls. I enjoyed providing care for the family, but the four months of hospice care really took a toll on me emotionally. I had done hospice care before, but not for that long and for someone I felt so deeply for.

It was not the death of my client that unearthed my suppressed pain. It was a note given to me shortly after from my 12-year-old daughter. The information in that letter is what opened the door for the pain, anger, and fear to return and consume me. I'll get to what was actually in that note later. That letter was the straw that broke the camel's back. It sent me into a deep depression followed by the panic attacks, and every medication you can name, I was on. I needed medication to sleep, and I barely ate anything. I self-medicated with drugs and alcohol, and ultimately, I got to the point where I couldn't leave my house. My sisters took my kids, and I was hospitalized.

That crazy whirlwind of events was a blessing. It shocked me straight. In the hospital I felt so overwhelmed. I felt my life had no real value and that every beautiful flower I had planted had been choked out by the weeds of my past. I felt empty inside, and I thought I had nothing to live for. I couldn't see how I had gotten to this place where everything had gone so wrong. My life didn't seem worth living. I felt like I was being overtaken by my life, and I needed to break out of the hold it had on me. I needed to get out. Get away from everything. I needed somewhere I could go and think clearly. I prayed and asked God to take me away. I asked that if it was His will, He would make a way for me to leave and start over somewhere else. I needed to break out of the picture to see things clearly. God made a way. He provided the money and closed all doors except for one. So in faith I walked through it.

No matter how much dirt you use to cover your trauma. Or how beautiful the flowers you plant in your life are, if you don't deal with the weeds at the root, they will always threaten to choke out the life you work so hard to make beautiful. It is only when you have to dig deep and pull those weeds out and expose them to the light, which is God's truth, that you can see the true beauty that helps to make up you and purges everything else.

18

I got settled in the new state and found another therapist, and after a year and a half of tear-filled nights, and many bottles of wine, I had written it all down. I wish I could say I felt relieved or a sense of accomplishment, but I just felt empty. I remember thinking, *now what?* What you are reading is a revised, cleaned up version of that purge. It is actually me in that analyzing stage we talked about earlier. As I went through the pages of emotions connected to my past, a lot of things became clearer. I've begun to see my life and myself clearly.

I want you to go on this journey with me because it is what made me who I am. I am not what happened to me. I am the overcomer of what happened to me. Some of the things you will read will be disturbing and a little hard to read, but remember the day is the brightest after you've gone through the night. You'll see the value in my life when you know the struggle. I implore you to join me on the journey, learn about me, learn about you, and witness the grace and guiding hand of God as we are going through. God be with us.

CHAPTER 2:
ABANDONED IN LOVE

I grew up without my biological mother or father. They were in the area, but they didn't directly participate in my upbringing. Their absence made a huge impression on me. I had a special bond with my mother. I think in some way all children do or at least want to. She was my she-ro. She was so beautiful, many people bragged to me about her. In my eyes, she could do no wrong. I was told a lot of horrific stories from gossiping people about why Social Services took my older sister and me from her. They said she would leave us with babysitters and wouldn't come back for days. She'd spend all that time in bars. I didn't remember any of those things. I remembered her as a loving mother always doting on me. It's funny what your heart allows you to remember.

The day Social Services came to our home, I remember how sad she was. It was genuine, and I could see her heart was breaking. I also remember my mother's last words to us, "Don't worry, I promise I'm going to get you back." She was never able to make good on that promise. I wasn't mad at my mother when we were taken away. I grew angry as time passed, and she made no attempts, as far as I could see, to get us back. She continued to have more children, and they were also taken away, some at birth.

When we first were taken from her, I knew she would get us back. I believed in her and wouldn't allow anything or anyone to change my mind. I longed for her so much that every knock at the door I heard, I thought was her. Every day when I got home from school, I hoped that she'd be there waiting to take me back home. I'd dream at night of her showing up at the foster home where we were at first or my grandmother's house, where we ended up staying and hearing her say, "Pack your stuff, I'm taking you home." I daydreamed about all the things we'd do together when I saw her again. I'd get mad with myself for trying to reason away the offense when she didn't show. Someone had to be holding her against her will, or maybe she didn't have a ride to come get me. Then I'd see people with their mothers and feel so lonely, so rejected, and discarded. I thought she said she loved me; why would she leave me?

I used to think it was sad because some of my siblings never got the chance to know her. Still, I realize now whether you get to spend time with your mother and create memories, or if you never know her at all, the longing is still the same. This longing can haunt you and keep you wondering, Is she thinking about me at this moment? Is she thinking about me on my birthday or Christmas? You continuously ask yourself questions that no answer will satisfy. Truly you just want to be with her, and you want her to want to be with you just as much. This longing made me feel crazy, angry, and lonely. It's those feelings of abandonment that created the mindset that I wasn't enough.

I wasn't enough to keep her with me. I didn't bring her the happiness and joy that she craved. I would wonder if she knew there was a hole in my heart that only her love could fill. I'd drive myself crazy wondering where she was. Who or what could be more important than being with me? I rode this roller coaster until I was about nine years old. It was then I gave up all hope for unification. I knew there was no way she was ever coming to get me. She had been convicted of manslaughter and sentenced to 10-20 years in prison.

That moment was like someone had dropped a whole building on me.

I had rejected everything everyone told me that contradicted the angelic idea I had of my mother. I rejected everything I had experienced that contradicted it. I had rejected everything I didn't want to believe about my mother and put her on a pedestal. After that moment, every horrible thing I tried to excuse away came to light. I began to remember every time she came over, but I didn't see her because she was getting high with my grandmother. I remembered how she would lie and say she'd still be there when I got home from school or that she'd be right back, and it would be months before I saw her again. I remembered all the times I saw her hurt people physically and emotionally. Everything I had turned a blind eye to had crushed every ounce of good I thought of her, and I saw her in a different light. I saw her as a liar, a cheater. I began to believe everything everyone had said about her. I developed a mindset that day. When people show you who they are, believe them. Don't believe better for them. Don't believe they can change. I started to see her not as a mother but as a murderer.

The last two paragraphs were from my first draft. I included them in conveying the true emotions I was feeling back then. When I originally wrote that, I felt the pain and hurt from the rejection, disappointment, and loneliness I experienced as a child. That nine-year-old girl came back to reclaim her victim status. She needed to be cuddled and told she was justified in her feelings. She wallowed in self-pity and traveled down memory lane, blaming every other horrible thing that happened after that on the letdown and absence of her mother. She stayed self-focused and self-centered as she explored how different her life could have been. How many opportunities she would have had if she'd had a better mother. Even reminisced about how she would have made better, smarter choices than her mother if given the same circumstances.

As I analyze the emotional outburst of that nine-year-old little girl, I see immaturity and lack of sympathy and empathy that she could not possibly have for her mother until she was actually in her shoes. I, too, had my first child before I was ready to parent. I was 16. I made the same choice my mother made, to give her up (to her father). He could give her the life I couldn't, I reasoned. I had nothing to offer her. I was living in a foster home, on welfare, and still in high school. I wasn't enough, and I couldn't see a way I could become enough at that time. My feelings of inadequacy weren't established because of her absence, they were passed down from generations, even in her absence.

I held a perspective of my mother that wasn't true. It was one I created in my mind by simply accepting the things I wanted to believe about her. Everything was revealed, but I filtered it, and I took in only what I wanted her to be. I created the mother I wanted in my mind and projected that image onto my mother. I never loved her. I loved the woman I had created in my mind. The problem with that is when she went to jail, I could no longer live in that imaginary place where she was perfect. Once the idea of what I wanted her to be—which was realistically unachievable for anyone—collided with the reality of the situations in that undeniable way, my world came crashing down. I was traumatized.

Trauma is caused when an action or situation doesn't line up with your previous assumptions of the person, world view, or situation. How often do we set expectations for people or situations in our lives and are disappointed in the reality of it because it doesn't line up with our expectations? Parents often do this with their children. As parents, we spend so much of our lives lovingly planning their lives, forgetting to take into consideration that our plan may not line up with their plan. Even though we feel we know what's best for them, we have to let them live their own lives and make their missteps.

What are some things you have envisioned that didn't line up with reality? Make a list of them, and next to each write the actual reality. Time is not a factor right now. Whether your vision is for the future or dealing with your past does not matter. The purpose of this exercise is to discover two things. One is to see if you can see the reality of the person or situation at all. If you can only identify your projected reality, you are headed for a rude awakening. The other is seeing both the reality and projected reality next to each other. This will provide a sense of what is real and what is not. I don't want to crush dreams. I believe in dreaming big, and seeing it is believing it. Still, I also know how important it is to see your dream as a goal, and facing reality is the best way to reach that goal. You can't achieve the dream until you have first faced, understood, and accepted reality. You'll know when you have faced it because you'll see the person or situation as it really is. Sometimes it may take a person you trust to point it out for you.

My mother wasn't the mother I needed. She loved me, but her love wasn't enough for me. I needed more. I needed a different kind of love than what she was offering. That's facing the issue. The details are not important because at the core of it, I wanted from her an idea of love she was not in a position to give. I used to say she should have been in that position before having children or gotten in that position after she started. That thinking is doing the opposite of facing reality and is judgmental. If we are getting hung up on should've, could've and would've, that's a clear sign that we're not facing reality. To come to any kind of true understanding, you have to be face to face with the reality of the situation. Once you've faced reality, you can gain an understanding from that reality.

My mother did love me. It wasn't the love I needed, but I can't deny she loved me. She came to see me on my birthday and would have what I called "birthday party in a bag." She'd show up with a bag full of everything needed for my birthday party. There was food, presents, and a cake. It didn't matter if I hadn't seen her all year, she'd show up on my birthday. It made me feel loved, considered, thought about. I understand now that she did love me even if it didn't look like I wanted it to. It was love, and it was from her. My mother could have felt like she wasn't enough for me as well. It wasn't because she didn't care that she let me go, it was because she cared so much. She wanted more for me than she thought she had to offer.

We want people to love us or show their love for us the way we expect, or we reject it altogether and feel like they don't love us. That's not true. Understanding everyone has their love language, and that situations look different from different viewpoints can give a better understanding of the reality of people and situations, or relationships. When I'm trying to understand something, I look at it from as many perspectives as possible before I decide the position I'm going to take. I don't want my feelings to interfere with analyzing the situation and getting a clear understanding, so writing it down is helpful. Something is sobering about looking at things in black and white. Your feelings are indicators, not determining factors.

When I lived out of my emotions—the pain and shame that came

25

with feelings of rejection—I was hurt, confused, and felt like I was not enough. After analyzing the situation, I could see she was someone who wasn't equipped to give me all the things I needed because she didn't possess them. But God had provided everything in His plan for my life to come together. I just had to see it to live in it. Once you have a clearer understanding, then you can move to acceptance. Don't misunderstand, acceptance doesn't mean agreement. It's an acceptance of reality. My mother wasn't able to provide what I needed as a child. The reason why it doesn't matter in the acceptance phase is because we've dealt with it in the understanding phase. Once you have an understanding, commit to it and move on.

I understand and accept the reality of that situation. That opened my eyes to see that God had provided, through many others, all the love I needed and more. He knew what I would lack when He placed me into that family; He made provisions for that. I carried a huge emotional weight being abandoned by both parents. I made a list of those people who made a difference in my life, whether they were in my life short term or long term. When I began to focus on all the people who helped me grow and learn along the way, I realized what I had gained was far more than what the people I had lost could have ever given me. God has a way of filling in the gaps in my life. I had allowed my emotions to steer my focus away from that fact and just didn't take time to notice. God will never leave you lacking. He wants us to be whole. But we can't see it if we stay stuck in our unreal expectations for people, situations, and relationships. It wasn't until I reached the acceptance phase that I could see it.

This is a framework that can be applied to many different situations. It's hard to understand the choices of others until you have walked in their shoes. Now that I see things from my mother's perspective, I not only understand, but I have a new respect for her. It's the same as adoption. Women place their children up for adoption, hoping that someone more capable of providing for them will love them and give them what they feel they lack. It doesn't always work out that way, but that is the intention. That was my mother's intention and mine too. The difference in our outcomes was that I had identified the root. It was too deep to pull out, but I chose to sever my connection with the lie that I wouldn't be enough.

I remembered that when my mother was away, all I wanted was to be with her. I didn't care what she could do for me. It was just her presence I needed. It was because my mother left that I knew the feeling of abandonment. I didn't want my children to experience that or form the mindset that they weren't enough. I decided I was going to do everything I could to show them that they were enough to make me deny myself and put their needs and wants first. The crazy thing is if I hadn't known the feeling of abandonment, I wouldn't have had the motivation to do what I needed to do to get my kids back. And I exposed that lie to the truth. I can do all things through Christ, who strengthens me.

There is a physical abandonment, but some have been emotionally abandoned. This occurs when a parent is physically present in the home but emotionally unavailable. I have experienced the effects of this situation, as well. The reason for the disconnect is irrelevant, whether it's a single-parent home and they are constantly working, or they are otherwise occupied with drugs and alcohol. Children need to be nurtured, cared for, and protected. I don't think my mother felt that in her childhood. I don't think my grandmother did either. Unfortunately, you can't give what you didn't have, so where did I get it from? Back then, I couldn't have even known to tell you, but now I see. "All things work together for good, to them that love God, to them who are the called according to his purpose" (Romans 8:28).

"Though my father and mother forsake me, the Lord will receive me" (Psalm 27:10 NLT). I received restoration as God showed me all the women He used to show me He was there taking care of me, loving me. Also, these women collectively set a standard for me. There are so many, but I had two amazing teachers in elementary school. Both just happened to have the last name, Williams. There has been a repeat of extraordinary people with that last name in my life. I don't believe in coincidences. These women went above and beyond their duties to show kindness that made me feel special.

CHAPTER 3:
UNCONDITIONAL LOVE

As I mentioned earlier, I lived with my grandmother after a short stay in a foster home. I wish I could say I knew her, but looking back now, I realize I don't really know much about her. My grandmother raised nine children of her own. By the time my sister and I moved in, she already had four other grandchildren living with her that belonged to one of my mother's sisters. I was just glad I wasn't the only one there because my grandmother was scary.

I thought she was nice at first. She spoke in a sweet voice and called me a baby. She was kind and attentive when I first arrived, and the social worker was there. But as soon as she left, she turned into another person. She warned me not to ever call her grandma again. I was to call her Ma or Mommy. After scolding me, she told me she wasn't going to call me by my given name Lillyan. From now on, everyone was going to call me Brooke. Then she sashayed down the long hallway that leads to the living room. I was in a state of shock.

On that first day at Ma's house, I felt like I'd entered an altered reality. Within the first hour and a half, I had been yelled at, threatened to have the piss slapped out of me, and stripped of my identity. It was a rude awakening that I wasn't ready for. I cried because I wasn't used to that kind of treatment, and I missed my mother. It had been a few weeks since I had seen my mother. I secretly hoped that being there gave me a better chance of seeing her. The one good thing was I shared a room with my cousin. She was older than me by six months but shorter than me, so everyone thought I was older.

In the beginning, I wasn't sure if she liked me because she laughed when Ma yelled at me for calling her grandma. She snickered and said, "She ain't been here one hour and already getting in trouble." I heard

Ma call her from the living room. When she came skipping back down the hall, she went into the kitchen. She grabbed a can of beer and stopped at the door of the room where I was. She said, "Ma wants you." I followed her to the living room. The large living room was furnished with a matching three-piece couch set. The sofa, loveseat, and chair were tan and black velvet and had cabins printed all over them, like in the woods. As I stood at the entrance of the living room, the chair was next to me on my left side. I was facing the loveseat, which was against the wall on the other side of the room. There was a glass coffee table with gold trim around it between the two, and the sofa was directly behind the coffee table.

In the corner between the sofa and loveseat was a black stand with 3 shelves. The stand had 3 pictures on each shelf. The pictures were of my aunts and uncles. Everyone was wearing a perfectly round afro. On the wall directly above the stand was a huge black and red picture on felt. It was a man's face, side profile, wearing an afro. Behind the sofa was a rectangular picture of a woman lying down on her side wearing nothing but an afro. As I looked around the room, I noticed a lot of statues of naked men and women in various poses. The room was a combination of gothic and dominatrix with a touch of family.

My cousin set the beer on a coaster. The coaster was on the coffee table in front of where Ma was sitting. Ma said, "Come here," motioning to me with her pointer finger. I advanced toward her, slowly stopping between the chair and the coffee table. She began to explain, "I didn't mean to upset you earlier. It's just that no one calls me grandma. It's either Ma or Mommy," she repeated in a slow seductive voice. "You are a pretty little girl. You look just like your father's people. You're the spitting image of 'em. I don't know why your mother named you after that girl; I told her I didn't like that name. I'm going to call you Brooke. Do you like that name?" I wanted to say, "No," but after what happened earlier, I was too afraid to say anything, so I just shrugged my shoulders. She said, "I'mma call you Brooke. I like that name for you." She opened her beer, poured it into a glass that was sitting in front of her on the table. She took a sip and sat back as if she was well pleased with herself. "Go ahead and finish getting settled in," she instructed while shooing us toward the exit.

That was the last time my grandmother called me pretty. From that day on, I was ridiculed, treated like a slave with no rights. We had to help cook and clean. I know that doesn't sound bad, but it was demeaning in every way. I remember my cousin and I were asked to wash some chicken that my grandmother was planning to fry. We had already had a training (that's putting it nicely) on how to wash a chicken. After washing it, we were instructed to lay the chicken on a foiled cookie sheet, which was the usual procedure. We had filled one sheet and were working on the other when Ma started fussing about the way we were laying the chicken down. I don't remember a training any time before on a specific way of laying the chicken in the pan. I guess this was it. She cursed and fussed, asking what we were doing. Of course, we stood dumbfounded and completely confused, and the next thing I knew, she was hitting us. There were fits and chicken flying everywhere. I ended up on the floor with a busted lip. For the longest time, I washed and laid chicken the way I learned that day. That trauma didn't become a teacher; however, it did become a constant reminder, and every time I fried chicken it haunted me. I don't fry chicken anymore.

Cleaning was the same. If it wasn't done right (Ma's way), there would be hell to pay. We had to wash all the walls in the house one day; it took us hours. My grandmother decided to wake us up at 4 a.m. to do them over, and we had school that morning. She was a night owl. She would stay up all night, sometimes for days at a time, getting high on crack cocaine. We referred to it as "having company," even if she was alone. We knew if Ma had company, she would at least be too busy to bother us. The downside of that was we wouldn't sometimes eat for days. During the school year, we would always ask other kids if they wanted their muffins or juice, so we could store up food for the weekends. For the most part, we always had food in the house, but we weren't allowed to help ourselves. The freezer had a lock on it, but honestly, even if it didn't there was a fear in us that only the deepest desperation for food could bypass. If it came down to it, we would sneak into the kitchen and steal food. That was usually how we made it through the summers.

The "we" I keep speaking of is four of us who shared a room. I had two more sisters who were added to the room with my cousin and me. My older sister who originally came to my grandmother's house with me went to live with her father. One of my sisters was left when my mother stayed with us for a brief period. A couple of years after, my other sister, who had been staying with her father arrived. It's complicated and not important right now. The point is we all shared a room, life-altering experiences, heartache, and so much pain. These experiences kept us together with an unbreakable bond of unconditional love. No matter what, I know I can depend on them. Our stories would fill an entire book that I do plan to write someday. I couldn't resist the chance to mention them. I pray they find the space and courage to one day write their own stories because even though we went through the same things as children, we all have a unique journey and different perspectives.

My tumultuous relationship with my grandmother left me with the most unanswered questions. Learning to sit in the discomfort of unanswered questions can have many outcomes. One is allowing your unsettledness to consume you. For some time, the thought of my grandmother would change my whole mood. I mean, my whole day would be ruined by the mention of her name. After my purge copy of this book, so many things surfaced. I began to rekindle hate for her from long ago. How could anyone be so evil, I'd wonder. It took a while, but I had to decide that I wasn't going to let her have that type of control over me anymore. If I continued to give her the power to change my mood, which would change my plans, I was allowing her to still control my life. This thought process changed my mindset. I had to become okay with not having all the answers to all my questions. I had to become okay with not understanding everyone and their choices and rationales.

I won't lie; this was hard for me. To stay the course, I often reminded myself that it was better than filling my heart with hate again. It was better than driving myself crazy trying to understand things that there were no words for. My grandmother stripped me of what little identity I had within the first few hours of our meeting. The question is why. That's an easy one. That's the first step to controlling and manipulating someone. After they take away your identity, they move to step two, giving you the identity they want you to have.

My grandmother did this in the form of abuse. She would call me every name in the book except a child of God. I was referred to as a bitch and a whore before I even knew what the words meant. I was 5, 6, and 7 years old being labeled and branded with names long before they were a normal part of my being. It makes you wonder. There was an equal amount of physical abuse used to reinforce verbal abuse. I believe some of the abuse we sustained was just Ma's way of relieving the stress and pressures of life. These things raise questions that will never have a proper answer because there isn't one. These questions are better left to the only one who can truly resolve them—the Lord.

Every unanswered question brought me closer to God. It was in Him I found the strength to love someone who didn't love me. I've found the strength to believe even when I can't see, and to continue to hope that people will want to be better and do better, even when they seem to be acting worse. I held on to these things when I was in a place so dark, I couldn't see, so lonely I couldn't speak, and where I was so afraid, I couldn't think. My first encounter with God Almighty showed me His saving grace.

Church with a family friend was a way of getting us out of the house on the weekends. I loved it! It was like a ray of sunlight shining through the dark cloud I lived in. I loved the church and learning about God and Jesus. We spent a lot of time at church on those weekends, and much more in the summer when we could stay throughout the week. One particular Sunday I was dreading going home. Because the weekends were so fun, it was becoming much harder to go back home on Sunday night. I was praying at the altar of the church. It was something the saints made all the kids do. They had us repeating, "Save me, Jesus." Over and over.

Before I knew it, the phrase resonated deeply within me. I didn't want to go back, and I wanted Jesus to save me. I wanted Him to come out of the sky and pick me up and take me with Him, so I didn't have to go back to that house, to that dark place. I prayed out of deep desperation to be saved that day. I told God I needed Him. I wouldn't make it without Him. I invited Him into my heart and my life. That day I had a supernatural encounter with the Almighty, and I returned to my grandmother's house changed. I was empowered and my strength renewed.

After my encounter I had this overwhelming urge to show my grandmother that she was loved. Every time I left the house and before bed, I would give her a hug, a kiss on the cheek, and say, "I love you, Mommy." I would make cards for her for no special occasion saying, "Thank you for taking me in." I felt if I showed her enough love, she would show us love. There were many times when this task was especially hard because the abuse didn't stop. Sometimes the love wasn't appreciated or reciprocated. I continued trying to show her love until I couldn't.

I was sitting in the doorway of my room. One of us would often sit there so we could hear if Ma called for us from the living room or we'd have to play security so her company wouldn't steal anything. Drugs make people very paranoid. My little sister, who was 3 or 4 years old at the time, was coming down the hall. I called her over, and we were laughing and hugging when my grandmother came down the hall. I'm still not sure what happened exactly, but one moment my sister and I were hugging, and the next I was on the floor, and my grandmother was stomping on my head. When I realized what was going on, I put my arm up to block my head, and when her foot came down again, she lost her footing and fell back into the wall. I used that moment to run into my room. I remember rocking myself uncontrollably in my bed and screaming into my pillow. I resolved that day that I couldn't love evil.

I hope that the previous emotionally-charged statement gave you some insight into my thought process. I was so close to the situation, I couldn't see anything else beyond my pain. Although many of them are, not all my memories of my grandmother were bad. I do remember some good times. Family sticking together was very important to her. Holiday parties, for a while, were at our house. She would get all the girls cooking in the kitchen; that's how I learned to cook. I remember she would buy us new clothes and shoes for school, and we'd get all decked out for Easter. She taught me to always look out for my sisters and never let anyone pick on them.

I taught those values to my children. I also remember that on Sunday mornings, she would listen to gospel music. There was one song she sang that became my favorite. It was "Rough Side of the Mountain" by Rev. F.C. Barnes. My grandmother would sing with so much passion, I could hear the sorrow in her voice. I felt like I understood her more through that song. Whenever I heard her singing, I started singing it with her, and one day she caught me. She was coming down the hall when she heard me; she stopped at the door of the room. She asked who was singing, and sheepishly I confessed. I couldn't carry a tune and really didn't know all the words. She took both my hands in hers and carefully pronounced the words so I could catch on. We sang that song together like we were on stage. From then on when it came on, she yelled, "Brooke, our song is on."

I know my grandmother is holding on to a lot of pain from her past. Being vulnerable and being strong don't go together in her world. I see it in her children as well. Talking about feelings was not something we were encouraged to do. It was a sign of weakness. Ma was the matriarch of our family. She was seen as strong. She could take on anybody in a fight—even men. She didn't take no mess; she wasn't afraid of anyone, and everyone knew it. She had many friends because nobody wanted to be her enemy. I've seen her cuss people out, then kick them out, and they would come back the next day. But under all that tough exterior is some deep-seated pain. I know that's why many people stay on the destructive path of self-medicating. They either believe it does not matter enough to seek out the issue or that they are not strong enough to face it. Drugs and alcohol have been the numbing agent for unresolved painful issues for too many years.

Currently, I don't hold any bad feelings toward my grandmother, just pity. I ask myself how someone so strong could be so weak. She allowed drugs and alcohol to dictate her moods, emotions, and life. If she has had a lot of hurt in her life, I don't think she sees herself as worth it or strong enough to stop the drugs and alcohol and face her past. Now that we've all left, she's lonely and continues to self-medicate. She's older but not much wiser. I do pray that her heart finds rest before she leaves this Earth. I believe her hurt is rooted in trauma from her own childhood. It reminds me of the little girl I had to release to the Lord. There's an emptiness she continues to try to fill, but only God can fill it. I pray she lets Him give her heart the rest it deserves.

CHAPTER 4:
STOLEN INNOCENCE

This is a hard chapter to write because I struggled on the path of forgiveness. I have made up my mind to forgive these people, but I find myself still being challenged while walking out the forgiveness. I don't want to cause pain by exposing anyone. However, if you know anything about my family, you probably have no trouble conjuring speculation on who is who. If that's your gig, then let it be on you. I'm more concerned that that person alone knows who they are and how what they did affected me.

I'm praying that the grace and forgiveness I extend to them will give them the courage needed to take responsibility for what they did. I pray they will seek the same grace and mercy that has freed me. I pray after a full revelation of the hurt and pain that was the result of these traumas done to me, they will want better for themselves. I pray they decide to turn away from the real author of these vicious deeds and turn to the Lord Jesus. He is the only Savior of souls. His grace and forgiveness are available to everyone, no matter their sin.

I don't believe in coincidences. However, I have always found it intriguing that all three of these men's names start with the letter J. I will refer to them as J1, J2, and J3. The order represents the timeline of my encounters, with some overlap. I'm a believer in getting the hard work done first, so when sitting down to write this book, this was my first chapter. The significance of the offenses impacted so many areas of my life. It changed the vision I had for my life and how I looked at and judged people who came in and out of my life. I admit I'm a deep thinker, and even simple things profoundly impact me. This thing, not being simple in nature, rocked me to the core. I struggled with real intimacy and had conflicts in the area of sexual relations because of it. I misunderstood because in these relationships I expected protection. Trauma occurs when reality conflicts with your expectations. It's an interruption of what you perceive as usual. A relationship that naturally cultivates an expectation of safety like a father or an older brother suddenly turning violent will cause trauma. Both relationships are expected to provide a level of security and care for you. The difference? A father is seen in a position above you, whereas a brother is seen as your equal. The brother understands your point of view, and you're basically in the struggle together. That was my initial perception of the relationship with J1.

I guess considering everything we were already going through, I expected more from J1. I looked at him as an older brother. I looked to him for strength because he was the male figure in the house and seemed to handle the things that were going on with style. He was the guy everyone wanted to be. He walked into a room and commanded attention. He was smooth, and all the girls wanted him. He was always dressed to the nines with a fresh haircut. Everyone knew him, and I was proud to be known as his sister. Even though we weren't really siblings, I felt like he was my older brother. We lived in the same house and were growing up together. I want you to understand the relationship I felt existed because it is the mistrust developed in that relationship that makes J1 stand out amongst the others. This incident shaped my future relationships with men.

It was a relationship that looted my innocence. I was a child who looked up to her big brother because of who she thought he was— strength despite adversity. You wouldn't guess our home life was as broken as it was looking at this kid. He was always so put together, an athlete, talented, and he danced like no one I've ever seen before. He was popular, funny, and an all-around nice guy, some thought. I'm not even sure how it started. I now know that there was prepping and priming. My formal education in psychology has opened my eyes to see the truth in some of the things he did. I previously thought they were big brother things. He would do small things like let me wear one of his hats for a day or slide me some candy when no one looking. These things that made me feel special were designed to manipulate me and make me feel like I owed him something. It worked. I thought we had a special bond because of those things, to the extent that when he started asking me to do things for him, I was happy to help. I wasn't excited about the things he wanted me to do. Still, as a child I'd think he probably wasn't thrilled about sharing his candy with me either, so I did them. I wanted him to feel special because he made me feel special.

It started off with helping with things like ironing a shirt or cleaning some sneakers, then escalated to a back massage and massaging other areas. There was something in those moments—attention and approval—that I was seeking to have fulfilled. There was the fear that if I didn't do what J1 said, he wouldn't like me or treat me special anymore. I hated doing the things he instructed me to do. As the nature of the deeds intensified, it became my goal to see the result of his happiness quickly, so it could be over. Even though that was the goal, I never left with a feeling of satisfaction. It got to the point I didn't want to do it anymore. I felt ashamed and grossed out, and the candy or whatever he had given me never eased those feelings. I started avoiding him as best I could, living two doors down from him.

I remember one night I was pretending to be in a deep sleep because I heard him in the hallway. He would come in the middle of the night and wake me up. I was tensed up in my bed lying motionless, anticipating him tapping me on the shoulder or leg, and when he did, I never moved. I even held my breath as he continued to try to wake me. I must have dozed off because I was awakened by one of the other girls getting back in the bed. I was relieved, but I'm ashamed to say I cried. That space, as disgusting as it was and how grossed out I felt doing it had once made me feel special. But that feeling was gone. I felt used and empty.

I'm sorry, this may be more than what some had bargained for. It was in this in-depth and painful assessment of my past that I began to understand why I made some of the choices I did in my future relationships.

There is a God-given need for humans to be in relationship with each other. It's how we were created. The trauma of this and other relationships in my past had distorted my view of relationships entirely. The way I felt cared for in the priming and prepping stage of this relationship was what I wanted. I was around 10 years old when this started. Because of my immaturity, I thought that was the only way to get what I wanted. If you wanted a guy to treat you special and give you attention, expect he wants sexual favors in return. That relationship had reduced my worth down to just sexual favors. This showed up in the clothes I wore and choosing to date guys who had money and could buy me things. I viewed sex as a means to an end. I wasn't on the corner prostituting, but there was little difference. A relationship formed with the sole purpose of financial gain is prostitution.

Now, I'm not being this transparent to get judged or dragged. I want the truth that I dug so deep to uncover to also help uncover some things for you. At least to encourage you to take a dive and find your own truth because getting to the root of the matter is how you deal with the problem and begin to change the unwanted outcomes. Don't misunderstand, I'm not blaming this for all the choices I've made. Still, the mindset that was cultivated here was used when discovering, attracting, and deciding on future relationships. I understood what I thought a relationship was supposed to look like. If I encountered anything that didn't fit that standard, I rejected it. I dismissed it because I didn't know how to deal with it. I rejected it because it didn't make sense to me. Either way, this mindset shaped my life.

What are some things in your life that may stem from a wrong mindset you created as a reaction to childhood trauma? Some mindsets are useful; they are not all bad. You can tell by their fruit. If you're still single (not married) and in your 40's, it may not be that there aren't any good men. I'm not suggesting that there is a problem with being single. I'm suggesting that you don't miss out on your man, if that's what you want, simply because you didn't do the work to change your wrong mindset first.

As I said, many things happen to cultivate this mindset. I thought J1 was, but he wasn't through with me. I had been avoiding him as much as I could, so I'm not sure how this encounter happened. I think I was too tired to fight when he woke me that night, and I used to imagine now how different my life would have been if I had. I'm not sure why it didn't seem like a big deal to him. I told him I didn't want to do it. It had never gone this far before. It hurt so bad, I thought I was going to die. In the past, when I would say I didn't want to do the things he wanted me to, he would talk to me and try to convince me it was the last time. This time he didn't care. He didn't stop when I said it hurt or cried. He moved forward like it didn't matter, like *I* didn't matter. When my cries got loud because of the pain, he put his hand over my mouth and kept telling me it wouldn't hurt so much if I would relax. There was no way I could relax.

He never tried anything else with me after that night. The next morning I was bleeding, as though I had gotten my period. I asked my grandmother what I should do. She said, "Ask the nurse at school for a pad." I didn't bleed anymore after that morning. I didn't even know what had happened that night until years later. I was agreeing with a friend that I was saving my virginity for my husband too. That was something I had been taught in church was a gift for your husband. They never explained precisely what it was, or what it looked like to lose it. My friend told me what she knew, and I was devastated. That day I found out through our conversation that that night my virginity had been stolen. I felt damaged and ashamed that I didn't even know. I thought no one was going to want to marry me now. I would be rejected on my wedding night as soon as my husband found out I wasn't pure anymore. Remember, I was a child.

Virginity has always been associated with purity, chastity, and innocence. I lost it all that day. I felt that J1 had gotten what he wanted, and I had been discarded. I didn't think about why he stopped pursuing me until that day. I was glad and relieved, but I never questioned it. I felt like that chapter in my life had ended, and I had put it behind me. But that day with this new realization, I felt robbed, manipulated, and so stupid. I hated him for doing that to me and myself for letting him.

I started to put pieces together in my mind, remembering J2 began during the time I was avoiding J1. I felt he probably put him up to it or told him that I let him, so he should try. So many things were becoming evident at that moment. J2 never went as far as J1, but he never primed or prepped either. He acted as if I was expected to know what to do. In my mind, they had plotted and planned against me. I decided on that day I wouldn't be used again; I'd be the user. I didn't plan to use men, but I established the mindset that there were only two options. You're either the user, or you will be used. There is no one "J" worse than the other; they all contributed to my stolen innocence. They all contributed to the development of these mindsets created.

J2, like J1, was a first cousin. He didn't live in the house with us, so we weren't close. There was no trust or relationship expectations as with J1. It always seemed like all expectation was on me. He acted like he had already done his part, and I owed him something. My grandmother would send me with him to pick up the money she was borrowing from someone to buy drugs from him. I didn't understand why she sent me with him; most of the time we picked up money from his mother's house. I hated doing stuff with J2; he smelled terrible and would always complain I wasn't doing it right. It was mostly on purpose. His arrogance repulsed me. It only happened a handful of times.

My grandmother would often send me out to pick up money with her drug dealers; J2 was the only one I knew. I had left with one of her dealers, and I thought we were doing the usual picking up of money. The ride started off weird because he never asked me where to go. He started driving and soon pulled over at a nearby park and parked the car, and we sat. I didn't say anything because he had a confused look on his face, and I was scared. He asked me how I was, and how old I was, I said okay, and 11. He sat for a few minutes more, then he quickly started up the car and drove me back to the house. He dropped me off and didn't come upstairs, which was the usual procedure. He sped off.

My grandmother opened the door for me and asked where the man was. I said, "He left." She said, "What do you mean he left. What did you do?" I didn't understand at first because I didn't do anything. It didn't occur to me until I had written it down. I didn't do anything, and that was the problem. I thought for the longest time that it was the guys, and that was just how guys are. I allowed that thinking to shape relationships. I hated to even suspect that of my grandmother, but it made sense. I concluded that I was being used, pimped out for drugs by my grandmother. It doesn't take away any responsibility from the J's actions. This clarified a lot for me.

I had allowed guys to treat me like a piece of meat all my life. I figure that was how guys were, and that was what was expected of me. I also believed the lie that I was in control of the circumstances, I was the user, not the one being used. I never thought that anyone else's relationships functioned any differently than mine had. This revelation changed my perspective on men but also on my grandmother. I didn't want anything to do with her after that. I stopped visiting her altogether, though my visits were already few and far between.

I thought about confronting her about it, but I knew I would never get the satisfaction I craved from that conversation no matter how it went. If she admitted it, I wouldn't know how to take that because I've always been able to keep a level of love and respect for her for the simple fact that she took us in when no one else would. I believe she did the best she could under the circumstances. That would just add insult to injury. I also felt that if she said no, I wouldn't really believe her, so to confront her would be fruitless either way. How did I reconcile this? We'll revisit this later.

My experience with J3 continues to haunt me from time to time. That was a huge event that I can't forget, no matter how hard I try. I remember it so thoroughly and vividly that the thought of him continued to paralyze me well into adulthood. Some things are so traumatic you bury them deep inside and can't remember them. I so wish this was one. I used to have flashbacks while with someone else, and I couldn't explain why I would suddenly be freaked out.

That day started off as a good day, which was not a regular occurrence in my childhood. It was a beautiful summer morning. I found a quarter while sweeping the porch and was going to treat myself to an Icee. I snuck downstairs to buy one from the Spanish family that lived on the first floor. The Icee wasn't entirely frozen solid, she explained, but I took it anyway. It would be perfect for me because I had to gobble it before anyone saw me. I got a pineapple one because they were out of my favorite flavor, coconut. I was conversing with the girl who had just sold me the Icee. I wanted to eat as much of it as I could before I went back upstairs, and I also just loved talking to her. She was much older than me, but we could always find something to talk about.

J3 saw me when he stepped out on his porch. He started commenting on my shorts and said he was going to tell Ma (nickname for my grandmother) I was out there trying to be grown. I ignored him at first, then on my way heading to the stairs, I stuck my tongue out and told him he should learn to mind his own business. My plan was to say that and run up the stairs. But he caught me and dragged me into his house and slammed the door. No one could have been home because I was screaming from the start and no one appeared.

The girl from next door was banging on the door; he didn't care. I wasn't sure what his plan was because he was jokingly taunting me, saying, "You going to tell me to mind my business." It turned serious very quickly. He laid me on the kitchen floor and put all his weight on me. He was a big guy. He played high school football, and I'm not sure what position, but he looked like one of the big guys they put on the front line. I was no match for him, but I still squirmed and screamed. He put one hand over my mouth and used the other to take off my shorts. I quickly became aware of his plan. I squirmed and tried to scream.

I could hear the girl from next door banging and yelling through the door. All the commotion stopped when he freed himself and thrust into me. My whole body went limp from the pain. After he said, "That didn't hurt." Crying, I said, "Yes, it did!" He said, "No, it didn't." Then he dragged me by my shirt and tossed me out the back door like trash. I was still shaking and crying, sitting on the back stoop when the neighbor I was talking to came around the corner. She tried to comfort me and advised me to tell my grandmother. I refused. I told her I would get in trouble anyway for being downstairs. I don't think she really knew what had happened in that house because she kept asking, "What did he do to you? I was banging on the door and trying to open it. I could hear you screaming." I didn't know how to respond to her questions. I knew I shouldn't have been downstairs in the first place. I felt it was my fault because if I was where I was supposed to be, it wouldn't have happened. I thought I deserved it for doing something wrong.

That's the mindset I developed that day. If you're doing something wrong, you deserve whatever happens to you. No matter how horrific. There was no measurement of the cause or effect. I was doing something I had no business doing. That made it my fault and made a bunch of other things that happened to me in my life my fault as well. I developed a mindset that excused people's bad behavior, considering my own contribution to the incident. I was so mad at him and felt there was nothing I could do about it. What could I have done differently in that situation to change the outcome? If I never snuck downstairs to get an Icee, it wouldn't have happened. I also developed a "do right or suffer the consequences" mindset. I began to expect bad things to happen to me because people were awful, my life was terrible.

I want you to understand that the first draft of this book was just a purging process. It was after I revisited the things I wrote with an analytic mind that I began to discover the root of these patterns of thinking I had repeated throughout my life. When you cultivate a mindset, your mind is literally set. Throughout my life, I had gathered information that supported that mindset and rejected everything else. That doesn't mean things didn't happen that were contrary to my mindset. I had chosen not to acknowledge them. It's like prejudice; you get a mindset about a group of people because of past experiences or what you were told. Because of your encounters, you think all the people in that set group are the same.

I had men in my life that were contrary to the Js, but I rejected the likelihood of it. I decided in my mind they were like them; I just hadn't seen that side of them yet. The anger I developed from my encounters caused me to have low expectations of men and I devalued them. They became worth nothing but what I wanted from them, and when they couldn't provide that or tried to offer more, they became expendable. I can't count how many relationships I fumbled or dismissed because he wanted more from me than I was willing to give. What I thought of them was directly connected to my own self-worth.

The important thing here is identifying the root of those mindsets and reversing them. Once I understood that all men weren't like that, I could then point out the supporting factors or the other men in my life who proved to be different. That allowed new relationships with men to be created on a new foundation that was individual and specific to each person. Also, when you're not expecting to be used and abused, you stop drawing those kinds of people to yourself. The scripture says seek, and you will find (Matthew 7:7). You will always see in people what you are looking for. What do you expect from people?

The problem then becomes trusting that those relationships aren't what the others were. This is where the 4th J comes in—Jesus. In my process of forgiving the 3 Js, God reminded me of 2 things. The first was found in 2 Samuel 13. I knew of the story of Amnon and Tamar from sermons I'd heard in the past. While reading it for myself, God revealed to me the power of unforgiveness. If I carried my torch of vindication, I couldn't see the hurt my unforgiveness caused others or the loss it had cost me. I had gone through life treating men badly because of what someone else had done to me. I lost out on real intimacy because they wanted a relationship that I couldn't even fathom. The men that wanted to give me more, I rejected.

I could finally see how continuing to be angry with the 3 Js caused me to be angry with all men and make decisions that continued to affect my relationships. I had to forgive them because it was going to destroy me. The second thing God shared with me was found in 1 Thessalonians 4:3-8. The author is warning the people of Thessalonica about abstaining from sexual immorality. In verse 6, it says the Lord is the avenger of these things. God was telling me to forgive them and trust Him to avenge any wrongdoing. This not only allowed me to forgive them but gave me the courage to expect good things from others, knowing God is my avenger. When I decided to trust God in this area, I felt a safety and protection that I had longed for and had never experienced before.

I want to apologize to anyone I have wronged while in my wrong mindset. I know hurting people hurt people, so I also extend forgiveness to the 3 Js. I believe if you woke up this morning, God is extending a hand of grace and mercy to you. I believe He can redeem you and restore you because He has done it for me and countless others. I pray your heart will be awakened to the good that lies before you and that you feel a desperation to take hold of it for your own sake. I used to believe that this is the way things are, and nothing is going to make a difference in my life. Don't believe the lies of the enemy. Choose to believe God can and wants to change your life, and He will.

J1, you had a promising future. God gifted you with talents for a purpose, and it's not too late. He can change your situation around. J2, I pray you begin to see clearly. I pray that clarity will allow you to recognize God's grace in your life, and you will know that He is what your heart is searching for. Nothing else will satisfy. Allow Him to fill the hole in your heart and give you a new purpose. J3, I pray God will rescue you from the grasp of the enemy. I pray you will come to rely on Him for your shelter, safety, and stability. I pray that you will rest in His unconditional love and that it will lead you and guide you in the way you should go. I want nothing but the best God has to offer for each of you and pray that you will accept it. In Jesus' name. Amen.

CHAPTER 5:
I DON'T WANT TO BE HERE

Ever since I can remember, I've struggled with being here. Here meaning in this world. I'm not sure if it's because I can't remember a time when I was just enjoying life. I came into a world of chaos, a family of dysfunction, and lived a life that had never reached the pinnacle of my lows. I find myself constantly thinking, will it get better? When will it be different? When will I find rest from the anxious feeling that continually haunts me? When will my life have purpose, meaning? Why is everything so hard? I'm tired of pressing forward when it seems forward only leads to a reward of more heartache. I must keep pressing. For what? I'm tired. I'm tired of trying and never getting ahead. I'm tired of one door opening only for the next to slam in my face. Trying leads to failure. Love leads to pain. Hope eventually leads to disappointment. I am tired of fighting this losing battle. I'm just tired. I wish I could just go to sleep and not wake up.

That was my thought process before I swallowed a full bottle of Tylenol. I was now in the custody of the Department of Social Services. I had run away from my grandmother's again. I told them if they took me back this time, I would kill myself. They didn't, but there I was with the same longing to be anywhere but where I was. I thought anything would be better than living at my grandmother's, but it wasn't. At least there I had my sisters to face the hell holes of life with. Here I had no one. No one understood me or even cared to try. They just gave me a key and an unenforced curfew. No one was there when I got played by an older guy, and my heart was broken. No one was there when the hood girls jumped me because I was new on the block. No one was there when I got caught in a gunfight and had to run for my life. There was no one I could talk to or confide in. I fought so hard to be free, never taking into account that I would also be alone.

The realization that the grass wasn't greener on the other side, it was just as brown, hit me hard. All my hopes for a better life were shattered, and I didn't want to go on. I wish I could say I felt better after I drank the charcoal, got my stomach pumped, and spent a week in a children's psychiatric hospital, but I didn't. I wish I could say that that was my last time trying to take my own life, but it wasn't. There were two more times. The feelings of desperation and despair had a hook in me that I could not shake. They lingered and cast a dark cloud over every aspect of my life until even good things were questionable. When good things happened, I'd be so focused on preparing for the imminent disappointment that was lurking trying to catch me off guard, I couldn't enjoy it.

I met a sister on my father's side I never knew. She wanted to be there for me, but it wasn't in the sisterly way I was craving. It was in a parenting way because she was about 15 years older than me. I did become very close to my niece, her daughter. She was younger than me, and I didn't feel like I could confide in her because of how she looked up to me. She didn't grow up the way I did, and she had her stuff together. She was gorgeous and a straight-A student. Her home life seemed perfect. She lived with her mom, dad, a little brother, and there was one on the way. Those were good things, but I couldn't see it.

I didn't take the time to enjoy or sometimes even notice the good things that were going on around me. This became a pattern in my life for a long time. I would seek and search for the bad in my life because that's what I was comfortable with. I could expect it, and it was what I was familiar with. I figured if I prepared for the worst, when it came I'd be ready for it. The truth is you'll never be ready for it. I expected and prepared for bad things to happen to me, and every time I was surprised. Even when I expected it, it was more than I had prepared for. It took me a long while to understand why and twice as long to change it.

When you fixate on something, it becomes all you can see. Some used to believe if you wanted something and you spent time meditating on it, eventually you'd get it. It was called the prosperity doctrine, a movement that some people still believe and practice today. I got caught up in that movement of calling things to me, so I thought. I got into the habit of meditating during my morning time with God. I would start off with worship and then go into a time of focusing on what I wanted. I would sometimes stare at my vision board and imagine myself doing all the great things I had put on my board. I would imagine living in the house I had thumbtacked up there and see myself in the vacation pictures lying on the beach. After a few minutes of that, I would pray and be in communion with God.

One day after my worship, I was feeling so good. It was that feeling of euphoria that you feel after being in God's presence. I sat down to pray, and God opened my eyes that day. He took a real situation I was going through at that time and brought to my attention some really good things that I had not noticed within that situation. He showed me all the good things that had happened around me that I did not see because of the nightmare of the situation I was dealing with. For the first time, I could see the good and the bad at the same time. Then He told me I had the power to choose what I wanted to focus on. It became clear to me that I had spent my life not only preparing for the bad, but focusing on the bad in my life.

I never realized that there was good and bad in everything because I had chosen for so long to focus on the wrong things in every situation in   my   life. I would always ask things like, "Why is it always something?" Or "How come nothing good ever happens to me?" and "What's next?" in anticipation of the next ridiculous thing to come about. This was a life-changing revelation for me. Unfortunately, my life didn't change right after. Even though I had this new knowledge, I had to put it to use to see what kind of difference it would make in my life. That's how you convert knowledge into wisdom, you use it.

I know now that I was experiencing depression and suicide ideation. But back then, I would spend a lot of time entertaining those thoughts. At the start of my day something small would happen.

50

Something as little as not being able to find something I needed. I am a planner, so I lay my clothes out for the next day the night before. In the morning I would misplace a sock and spend 20 minutes looking for that sock. But wait, that would just be the beginning. Then I'd be late, and everything from that point on would be an addition to my already bad day.

The sun could be shining brilliantly in the sky. The air could be warm with a skin-kissing light breeze. A whole caterpillar could have emerged from its cocoon right in front of me, and I would not notice any of it because I had already declared my day a bad day when I couldn't find my sock. The point is to show the slippery slope that our thoughts can lead us down. Once I realized I could choose between the good and bad of situations, every time I would choose the bad, I'd beat myself up about it. I'd say, "You're so stupid," "If you know better, you are supposed to do better," and my favorite, "What is wrong with me?" For the longest time, I thought this was all my doing.

The truth is the reason it's so hard to change your thoughts and behaviors is because you are going against something. Think about it like this. Let's imagine you were trying to push something. Something that we would think would be impossible to move, like a car. You're looking at this car and thinking, I can't move this. It's the same with your thoughts. You're thinking, This is how I am. I can't make myself not have these thoughts. Let's go back to the car. The car is in a position, and you want it to change. The first thing you need to do is reverse the position. What's keeping the vehicle in this position? The gear, so change it from park to neutral. It's the same with your thoughts. I keep having these negative thoughts. I want to change. When a negative thought comes into your mind, recognize it, then transform it into something positive. Instead of fixating on my lost sock that morning, I could have thought, It must not have been meant for me to wear those today and got another pair. Intentionality is the key. I had to stop letting my thoughts just happen and think to control my thoughts. Just like moving the car. Some thinking had to be done to figure out how to move the vehicle, but once you changed the gear to neutral, you could move it with more ease. Seems easy? It's not.

It's not as easy because I've been in this habit for a long while. The longer that car has been sitting there, the harder it is to move, even in neutral. The longer I had been thinking like this, negatively, the longer it was going to take to develop a positive thought pattern. I had been thinking that way my whole life. I got that revelation about 20 years ago, and there are still times when I have to remind myself that I have a choice and can think good positive thoughts or negative thoughts. Don't feel hopeless or think it's fruitless. The key is to remember you have a choice.

I realize now when I start thinking that way, it's usually associated with the people I'm around. When I'm around people who are stuck in the same place, their conversation is laced with negativity. Too much time with them could have me entertaining that thought process again. You might say then why do you hang out with people like that? First, it reminds me of where I once was. You get such a feeling of gratitude when you see how far God has brought you. Second, I can remember what it felt like and what my life looked like when I thought that way. Not only does it push me to keep trying no matter how many times I stumble, but it urges me to let others know it's possible. It's not impossible to change your thinking. You don't have to live that way forever. That's not just how you are. It can be different. You can get better. I know because I'm better and improving day by day.

I do understand that there can be a biological component to depression, and medication can be of assistance. But like I stated earlier, this is based on my experience, not my educational background. There is something to be said about the effectiveness of Talk Therapy. After three suicide attempts, a diagnosis of agoraphobia, and bi-polar disorder, I have been on almost every psychotropic medication there is. I was on medication for my problems and medicine for the side effects. Sometimes 8-10 pills just in the morning. I was dependent on these meds. I would say things like, "The world can't handle me without my meds." The truth was I didn't want the world to see me without the crutch of my pills. The pills and my diagnosis became my identity. I was that girl suffering from depression and needed all these pills. I didn't have to be responsible for my actions or my thoughts. I liked it that way; it was how I was most comfortable being in and known by the world. Even if it wasn't right. I lived in this lie because it was convenient and easier than facing the truth.

I really was responsible for my actions, my thoughts, and my life. How I showed up in the world was my responsibility and choice. I had to take the mask off. Stop hiding behind the pills and diagnoses. I had to be who I wanted to be, not just who I was. That phrase, "that's just how I am," aggravates me because I know it's a cop-out for lack of trying. I'm not against mental health medication. If it weren't for that, I would have never made it to the point where I realized I didn't need it to face my problems. I told myself I was dependent on it. There were no real practical steps to getting off medication for me. I just stopped taking it. As a professional, I know there are real risks when doing that, and I am not advocating for anyone to stop taking any medication without medical supervision. But I did.

I started fasting and just stopped taking them. During that fast, I became open and vulnerable with God in a way I never had before. I allowed God to work in me and reveal things to me about myself that I never realized. My conversations with God allowed me to see myself through His eyes. I began to understand I had a purpose, and that I was never alone. God has been with me every step of the way. I learned I could always lean on Him for anything, big or small and that He would still be right there where He has always been. Now I'm dependent on God. The point is for you to have your own conversations with Him. I know it will change your life and your perception of your life like it did for me.

CHAPTER 6:
I AM WORTH IT! ARE YOU WORTH IT?

Identifying the wrong mindsets and changing my thought patterns changed my life. The parts of my life that weren't fruitful are now turning around; it's never a finished work if we do it right. One part of my life that was not bearing good fruit was relationships. Not just intimate relationships but all of them. I was a people pleaser. I wanted everyone to like me. I never wanted to stir the pot, so to speak. That's one reason I kept so much pain and anger inside. What if people really knew? What would they think of me? How would they view me? I always wanted everyone to see me as someone good. Followed the rules. Didn't make trouble. That got me nowhere. It made me bitter. I started feeling like everyone just wanted to use me for one thing or another. In my mind, everyone had ulterior motives for hanging out with me. I was very distrustful of people.

Unfortunately, the majority of the time, people proved me right, but that's because as I said before, you will always find what you are searching for. The Bible says the eyes are the window to the soul (Matthew 6:22-23). The things that you acknowledge or stand out to you in other people are a reflection of what's in your own soul. I used to think everyone was jealous of me. It turned out I was the jealous one. Beware of definitive words like everyone and always; they are an indication of soul projection.

You will see the picture the way you believe it to be until you change your viewpoint. That's why it is so important to write it down. Writing it down is how you step out of the picture. Looking at the image of your life from the outside allows you to ask yourself the hard questions. What does that thought mean to me? Where did that thought begin? What did it stem from? What other areas of my life has it affected? How has it hindered my progress? What can I learn from it moving forward? The answers to these questions will help to answer questions specific to you, like Why do my relationships fail? Why do I keep choosing these types of partners? Why am I an overachiever? Why am I an underachiever? Why am I so anxious? Why can't I sit still? Why don't I have any motivation to change the things I know are not right in my life? Analyzing your life, especially the traumas, will provide the foundation you need to change, giving you a better perspective.

Changing your wrong thoughts or mindsets is the next step. In the chapter, "Abandoned in Love," it was when I was in the same position as my mother that I had a more comprehensive perspective of the reasoning behind the choices she made. By putting yourself in another person's shoes, you can gain some insight into what they might have been thinking. Hopefully, you'll gain some empathy for their position if nothing else. Trying to understand instead of criticizing and judging helped me forgive my mother. It taught me the most important part of being a parent is sacrificing for your children. God sacrificed His Son for us. What are we willing to sacrifice for the ones we claim to love? That doesn't just apply to parent-child relationships. Can we sacrifice our time or being right all the time? Can we sacrifice our money, or are the things we want more important than the things they need? Many other questions can be asked, but the most important one is, can you say you truly love someone if you're not willing to sacrifice for them?

The Word says, "Love your neighbor as you love yourself." How much do you love yourself? I didn't love myself for a long time. I came to realize that when I analyzed my relationship with my grandmother, she never really loved herself. When you love someone, you want them to be healthy—mind, body, and soul. We make our children eat their vegetables and take medicine because we want their bodies to be healthy. We make them go to school and do their homework and read to them at night because we want their minds to be healthy. We celebrate their birthdays, their great report cards and reward their good behavior because we want them to know they are special and mean a lot to us. We encourage them to stay away from things that will hurt them because we love them. Whether we do these things for ourselves or others, they are all actions of love.

My grandmother's actions showed me she didn't love herself, and therefore, couldn't teach anyone else how to love. When I learned I didn't love myself, I turned to God to show me what real love looks like. I understood why God told me to show her love as a counter to the abuse. Showing love causes the heart to soften and teaches others how to love. I don't think she doesn't know; I just think that her indulgences have a great hold on her. There are things we need, and things we want; keeping them balanced is loving. It's not an emotion or butterflies in someone's stomach. Loving someone can be motivated by passion, which is a feeling, but love is an action. It has to be acted upon or experienced. Love is not something you feel, it's something you do. You can't say you love someone unless you are willing to sacrifice for them. This is just the surface of the things I was able to uncover during my analyzing process. I'm still receiving new revelations about myself today.

I have only touched on a few things I've learned about myself through the analytical process, and there are so many more. I could take each trauma I shared with you and write a whole book of the things I've discovered within that one thing. The great thing about writing it down is you can always refer back to it. It wasn't until I could see how the sexual abuse from my past had affected me that I could identify the brokenness in my own intimate relationships. When I was ready to settle down, I couldn't for one reason or another. I knew it wasn't all me, but I recognized I was the common denominator, and I was the only one that I could control. I had to change my approach. The way I thought about men, which stemmed from my past trauma, inhibited me. I had to change my thinking about men, which would automatically change my approach.

In the beginning of this book I told how this journey started; I received a note from my daughter. That note opened up wounds that I had let heal over without cleaning them out first. I was already in a sad place because of the passing of my client. The note took me over the edge. In this note from my daughter, she explained something that happened to her. It left her with the same confused, unprotected, uncertain, unloved, and disgusted feeling that I had only felt at one time in my life. My emotional state went right back there.

I was not able to be there for my daughter emotionally. I did all the supportive physical things. I believed her; I took her to all the doctor's appointments.

I did all the court things with her, but emotionally I was unavailable because I hadn't dealt with my own emotions concerning my sexual abuse. I had masked it all with the easiest masking emotion, anger. I was mad at her father for his stupidity. What was wrong with him? Why would he do this? I was mad at myself for not protecting her. How did I miss this? I should have known. I was mad at his family for the way they started treating my children. It wasn't her fault. She didn't do anything wrong. I thought they were her family too.

This incident gave me the push I needed to deal with the things I had let it fester. That's where generational curses come from. When we sweep things under the rug and act like they didn't happen, they will keep happening. Sexual abuse, especially in African American families, has been swept under the rug for too long. Why are we so adamant about protecting a grown man? Especially one that has hurt a child. Why would a child be made to feel like an outcast while the adult is accepted and protected? That seems backward to me. But it happens all too often. It happened that way with me, and unfortunately, it happened the same with my daughter.

I don't have to imagine myself in her shoes because I've been in them. But if you (those who continue to act like it didn't happen) did, you would see the scared child that wasn't validated, comforted, and protected by people who said they loved her. It's a crushing blow to areas of trust, security, her ability to identify love, and it's all masked by the easiest masking emotion—anger. The demons we don't slay will be passed down to the next generation. I may have done everything I was supposed to do, but I wasn't the emotional support she needed back then, and for that, I'm sorry. I want to be there for my kids in every way possible. I don't want my unresolved issues to hinder my parenting as they once did. That's one of the reasons I continue to work on myself every day. I want to go first so they will not be afraid to follow. They are worth it. I am worth it. Are you? Are your children or future children or the children that God places in your life to influence worth it?

CHAPTER 7:
CLOSING

I want to thank you again for taking this journey with me. I hope you have gotten something out of it. I know it was a lot. Really, it's not even the half of it. I have been through a lot, and I refuse to leave any lessons behind, so I'll continue to go over my life and share them with anyone interested. I have so much more to share. I'm praying that my vulnerability and transparency will inspire someone. Letting people know that they can still have life and have it abundantly no matter what has happened in their past.

If I have stepped on your toes or made you feel ashamed, I hope this was an eye-opener and that anger doesn't mask your true feelings. I pray that the truth shall set you free from your shame. Things don't need to be forgotten to be forgiven. It's actually the opposite. If you want to be forgiven of something, you should acknowledge it. I love everyone with the love of God. Thank you, and I hope you will join me next time.

Made in the USA
Columbia, SC
07 July 2021

41527455R00035